a
fatherless
generation

ZADORA COVINGTON

a
fatherless
generation

TATE PUBLISHING *& Enterprises*

A Fatherless Generation
Copyright © 2011 by Zadora Covington. All rights reserved.

No part of this publication may be reproduced, stored in a retrieval system or transmitted in any way by any means, electronic, mechanical, photocopy, recording or otherwise without the prior permission of the author except as provided by USA copyright law.

The opinions expressed by the author are not necessarily those of Tate Publishing, LLC.

Published by Tate Publishing & Enterprises, LLC
127 E. Trade Center Terrace | Mustang, Oklahoma 73064 USA
1.888.361.9473 | www.tatepublishing.com

Tate Publishing is committed to excellence in the publishing industry. The company reflects the philosophy established by the founders, based on Psalm 68:11,
"The Lord gave the word and great was the company of those who published it."

Book design copyright © 2011 by Tate Publishing, LLC. All rights reserved.
Cover design by Amber Gulilat
Interior design by Nathan Harmony

Published in the United States of America

ISBN: 978-1-61346-106-8
1. Religion / Christian Life / Personal Growth
2. Self-Help / Spiritual
11.06.24

Dedication

To my heavenly Father, You filled a void that nobody else could.

Acknowledgements

First and foremost, I must acknowledge you, heavenly Father, because you gave me the mandate to write for you and only you. Without You, Father, I'm nothing! I love you! I thank you for all you do!

Next, I want to acknowledge my husband, because he has truly been a father to our children. He is showing our sons what a real man does and that is father your children. Thank you for being a great husband and a great father. I love you!

I would like to give thanks and appreciation to the Tate family; you truly have made my heart glad. God bless you!

I truly want to thank every man that has stepped up to the plate to be a dad to their children and the children around them who don't have a dad in their lives. Thank you for spreading a legacy of the gospel to our future. God bless you richly!

Last but not least, I truly would like to thank every man for accepting your true calling, and that's being a father to your children. If you accepted your mandate as a father, I personally thank you! Thank you for being there for your children and know that your children do need you in their life. God bless you!

To my three beautiful children; well, what can I say? I love you more than words will ever say! You are truly a gift from God!

I dedicate this book to my mother, who tried to father me the best she could. Mother, truly I thank God for you! You are the best mother in my world! I love you! You will always be my number one queen!

I want to dedicate this book to my husband of fourteen years; thanks for fathering our three beautiful children! I thank God for you! I love you!

Table of Contents

Introduction
~ 11 ~

The Fatherless Children
~ 15 ~

Faith through the Fire
~ 31 ~

The Bigger Picture
~ 41 ~

Behind a Smile
~ 49 ~

Carnality vs. Spirituality
~ 59 ~

A True Heritage
~ 71 ~

The Father's Unfailing Love
~ 85 ~

No Condemnation
~ 93 ~

Introduction

My purpose in writing the first chapter was just to share a little bit about my struggles of not having a dad, but this book is mainly to everyone who has a void inside of them because they didn't have a dad in their life and sought the world to fill that void. I want to lead them to their true father the heavenly Father. This book is also for that person that wants to know more about the love of the Father and what it truly means to trust the heavenly Father. If you open up your heart to the Father and surrender unto Him, you will receive what you are looking for when you open up this book. This day was ordained by God for you to receive your breakthrough. My prayer the whole time I have been writing this book is, "Father, place this book into the hands of the people predestined to read this book for a divine appointment with you." So if you have this book in your hands, I know that the Father has predestined it so. Open your heart and surrender your will. Allow the Father to have His way in you. He loves you and wants to father you!

In this book I talk about my struggles of not having a father in my life and how it affected me. I'm writing about being left fatherless. The issue of children growing up without their dads in their life affects many children. Most of the children that grow up without a dad struggle with many issues such as rejection and condemnation. This book gives strength to the fatherless; it shines the light on hidden issues and persuades the fatherless to put their trust in the heavenly Father. This book gives instructions on how to live a spirit-led life and not a carnal lifestyle. If you don't know who you are in the heavenly Father, you will know once you read this book. This book gives insight about the heritage we as children of the heavenly Father have when we are His children. The heavenly Father is our only true hope; He is our true Father. My prayer is that the heavenly Father places this book into the hands of the people predestined to read this book for a divine appointment with Him. Romans 8:28 (kjv), "And we know that all things work together for good to them that love God, to them who are the called according to his purpose."

Blessings,
Zadora Covington

A Word to My Dad

John,
I want to let you know that I have forgiven you for all things you did to my family. I want you to know that I love you. Where ever you are if you do get a chance to read this book, know that you are forgiven and if you want to reach me you can.
    Your daughter,
    Zadora Stringfellow Covington

The Fatherless Children

With the baby-booming years came pre-marital sex, drugs, and alcohol abuse, a free-for-all kind of attitude that led to many babies being born without a father in their life. In today's society there are many children without their fathers, whether it was because the men never had a father in their life to show them how to be a father, or they just decided not to have that relationship with their children.

Another reason for the fathers not being in their children's life is because of premarital relationships; it leads to children being born out of wedlock. The mother doesn't know who fathered her child, or the father denies being the father of the baby, or the mother refuses to allow the dad to have a relationship with his child. The end result is the father isn't there for their children.

The child is the one most affected by the severed relationship not the parents. The children are deprived from ever having a thriving loving father, son, or daughter relationship. I was searching the internet to find some facts on how many children are without their father due to premarital sex, divorce, abuse in a relationship, or other causes for a child being left fatherless. The percentage of people who have premarital sex not thinking about the consequence is alarming.

Many people don't think about the end result of their actions. Whether its premarital relationships or marriages that end in a divorce, the child is left suffering; they either lose their mother or their father or both parents. The child is the one who will ultimately struggle with feelings of rejection. Due to the absence of their father, they will have a void that no one can feel.

According to a synopsis done by Lawrence B. Finer, PhD. at publichealthreports.org, there are many Americans who have pre-marital sex that led to children born out of wedlock, therefore left fatherless.

> Results: Data from the 2002 survey indicate that by age twenty, 77% of respondents had had sex, 75% had had premarital sex, and 12% had married; by age forty-four, 95% of respondents (94% of women, 96% of men, and 97% of those who had ever had sex) had had premarital sex. Even among those who abstained until at least age twenty, 81% had had premarital sex by age forty-four. Among cohorts of women turning fifteen between 1964 and 1993, at least 91% had had premarital sex by age thirty. Among those turning fifteen between 1954 and 1963, 82% had had premarital sex by age thirty, and 88% had done so by age forty-four. Conclusions: Almost all Americans have sex before marrying. These findings argue for education and interventions that provide the skills and information people

need to protect themselves from unintended pregnancy and sexually transmitted diseases once they become sexually active, regardless of marital status.

Children born from 1960 to 1981 were called Generation X. I was born in 1975. I was already born into a generation that was labeled a lost generation from the world. The Generation X children were products of divorce or pre-marital relationships that birthed children into the world without their fathers. I was born into a pre-marital relationship that was full of abuse. My father abused my mother and siblings on many occasions. My mother endured abuse at the hands of my dad before and after I was born.

Finally, God gave my mother the strength to leave my dad after many accounts of him abusing her and my siblings. With the help of God we safely got away from my dad. The last time I ever talked to him was on the phone when I was a little girl; he called my great-grandmother's house from the county jail. He promised me that when he got out of prison he would find me. I never have seen or heard from him since; he was gone out of my life that quickly.

Growing up as a child I felt a void in my life not having a father in my life; I had no father who could call me daddy's little girl. What my daddy did to my mother and siblings was wrong, and God helped me to forgive my dad and others that mistreated me because of what my dad did to my mother and siblings. God helped me to know that I wasn't to blame for what my dad did. I had blamed myself for many years. I used to think, *What if my life was normal like others?*

I pictured having an all-American family, where I could sit on my daddy's lap and he would listen to me talk about my day at school, my worries, my fears, and he would reassure me that he would protect me and not let anyone hurt me. I needed him there to shield me and protect me. I just wanted to be daddy's little girl, his little princess. Even though I was angry with him, I still yearned for him to be in my life. You see, every child wants to have a daddy that they can depend on. Growing up without my dad in my life left a void that no man could fill but him. I went through a stage of life feeling unloved, unwanted, rejected, left out, and confused.

When I was a teenager I sought love from relationships, but the guys I dated couldn't give me the love I sought after. They couldn't give me the love I needed and desired—a father's love. I thought that they could fill that void; in reality I really didn't want to be with them, I just wanted to be loved and accepted by my dad. As a child I remembered what my father told me, that he was coming to get me when he got released from prison; I held on to his words. I cried many days for the love of my dad. I waited and searched for him. Growing up, I always prayed that my dad would come find me, because I wanted him so badly to be in my life. My dad missed out on every special occasion in my life, all my birthdays as a little girl, as a teenager, and as a young adult. He missed out on my senior prom night, my graduation day, my wedding day, and the birth of his grandchildren.

My wedding day truly was a special occasion that I wanted to share with my dad. I wanted him to be at my wedding and walk me down the aisle. I wanted to hear the preacher ask who gives this woman to this man to marry; I wanted to hear my dad say, "I do." My dad has missed out on every important day of my life. The absence of my dad caused me much pain. I struggled with feelings of not belonging; I felt that I didn't have an identity.

It hurt me that I didn't know who my dad's family was; I never got to meet my dad's parents. I always questioned if they even knew I existed. I needed to know who I was, what my heritage was. I struggled with all kinds of thoughts. The more I contemplated on not having my dad in my life, the more it caused me to be depressed. I cried many days; the more I searched for my dad, the more disappointed I became when I couldn't find him.

In 1996, my life was changed; the day I accepted Lord Jesus into my heart it was a start to a new relationship between a daughter and her heavenly Father. You see, I didn't know that the day I accepted Jesus Christ into my heart was the day I became the heavenly Father's daughter.

Romans 8:17 (NIV) says, "Now if we are children, then we are heirs—heirs of God and co-heirs with Christ, if indeed we share in his sufferings in order that we may also share in his glory." I was adopted into a royal family through the blood of my Lord and Savior, Jesus Christ. I was predestined to be a child of the most high God from the beginning of time. Romans 8:28 (KJV) says, "And we know that all things work together for good to them that love God, to them who are the called according to his purpose."

That's when God told me he had a purpose for my life. God allowed my dad not to be in my life for a reason. If my natural dad would have stayed in my life, my destiny would be polluted, corrupted by him. I wouldn't be writing this book if my dad was still in my life. God is in the business of using the painful issues in your life to minister to others. My dad couldn't teach me what I needed to know, only my heavenly Father could. He couldn't nurture me the way my heavenly Father does. God had a plan for my life.

God allowed me to be without my dad, because he knew that there will be many children without a father. Those fatherless children need to know that God loves them, He is their father, and He understands everything that they are going through and have gone through. I didn't know that God had a greater purpose for me to write to the unreachable to help led them to Christ Jesus their deliverer.

My dad was moved out of my life so that God could father me into my destiny. My heritage was not with my dad, but with my heavenly Father. I had to learn how to walk in my correct heritage. I was a princess being groomed into my destiny, into my purpose, into my calling by my heavenly Father, the King of Kings and Lord of Lords. Romans 8:29–31 (KJV) says,

> For whom he did foreknow, he also did predestinate to be conformed to the image of his Son, that he might be the firstborn among many brethren. Moreover whom he did predestinate, them he also called: and whom he called, them he also justified: and whom he justified, them he also glorified.

God knew my destiny even before I walked in it, even before I accepted it. My heavenly Father knew I needed him more than I needed my dad. Shekinah Glory, a gospel choir, sings a song that says "Father, wrap me in your arms and father me." The first time I heard that song, it ministered to me. I got an understanding of what my heavenly Father wanted to do in my life and through my life. All along he wanted to father me. He wanted to father me into my destiny, my purpose. He wanted to use me for His purposes. He wanted to love all my hurts away. The day I was saved by grace through faith in Lord Jesus was a start of a new beginning for me. It was the beginning of me walking into my true identity, me being God's daughter.

It took me a while to truly open up my heart to my heavenly Father. Because of not having a father, I struggled with trusting, leaning, and depending on God as my Father. I had trust issues because my dad let me down. I was born into a life where all I had seen was the man I called daddy beat and abuse my mother, sister, and brother. Trust was something I felt had to be earned. It was hard to put my trust totally in my heavenly Father. I couldn't truly receive love from God, because I didn't know how to and why He loved me. I had to learn how to rest in his bosom trusting and depend on Him. I had to learn how to receive His love.

Because I never had a father-daughter relationship, it was hard for me to accept the love that my heavenly Father was giving me. The only memories I have of me having a father-daughter relationship with my dad were memories of a hostile environment full of abuse and anger. The issues in my past caused me to build a wall in my life; I couldn't trust anyone because I didn't want to be hurt anymore.

I had people come in and out my life. That was one thing I struggled with, thinking God would leave me. I felt I would be alienated from Him just like I was alienated from my dad. I cried out to my heavenly Father to bring my dad back into my life, but God was all I ever needed. I didn't know that God had been here all along, even before I had a personal relationship with Him. He was with me, protecting and shielding me from the hands of my enemies. God's unfailing love covered me and healed all the bruises of my broken heart.

The more I sought my heavenly Father's love and security, the more His love conquered all that I had harbored in my heart against my dad for alienating me. The peace of the heavenly Father overshadowed me. I didn't understand that his love was so great for me that even when I disappointed Him, He still wooed me back with his love. I realized who I truly was: the daughter of the Most High God.

I had to learn to come to the heavenly Father about everything; no matter how minute or how big, the heavenly Father is concerned with everything about me. The same way a child goes to their dad is the same way we must come to our heavenly Father, trusting in Him. He is concerned with everything that we go through. Only the heavenly Father can do what my daddy couldn't do. Man has limitations, but our heavenly Father has no limits. God is omnipresent, omniscient, and omnipotent. He's always *present*, He's all-knowing, *and He is an all-powerful God.*

God removed my dad out of my life because he knew that I deserved so much more, and my dad couldn't give me what my heavenly Father could. The transition from being without a dad to being fathered by God, my heavenly Father, was predestined before birth. I was pushing away the one who loved me more than I loved myself. God showed me great love, unconditional love, because He gave His only Son on the cross for my sins.

As a child, I felt God tugging at my heart but didn't know how to come to him. God knew that the absence of my dad in my life would draw me close to Him, and it would be my testimony to many to help Him minister to the brokenhearted, the fatherless, and the ones that need healing and deliverance. God is using my life to help others, and He wants to use yours if you are willing to surrender unto Him; we must be a willing vessel and fit for the Master's use. We must trust God that he knows what's best for us. We must allow him to lead us into our destiny. I was a bruised marred vessel, but God made me new, and He healed me.

Jeremiah 18:1–6 (KJV) says,

> The word which came to Jeremiah from the LORD, saying, Arise, and go down to the potter's house, and there I will cause thee to hear my words. Then I went down to the potter's house, and, behold, he wrought a work on the wheels. And the vessel that he made of clay was marred in the hand of the potter: so he made it again another vessel, as seemed good to the potter to make it. Then the word of the LORD came to me, saying, O house of Israel, cannot I do with you as this potter? saith the LORD. Behold, as the clay is in the potter's hand, so are ye in mine hand, O house of Israel.

When a person is making pottery, they first must prepare the clay by wedging it to remove all air bubbles before putting the clay on a wheel to form a design out of the clay. The clay starts out as a ball; while the clay is being formed, the potter must keep his hands wet so that the clay will be able to be move around freely on the wheel to form the image that the potter is trying to form. The potter uses their hands to keep the clay centered on the wheel and to keep it from falling off the wheel. The potter puts their finger in the middle of the clay to create the inside of the bowl or vase.

The potter works on both the outside and inside of the clay in order to form a beautiful piece of art. The potter uses a kiln, to remove carbon and other impurities that can cause problems. The kiln is also used to harden the clay so that the potter can handled it to color and glaze the clay more easily so that the potter want warp or crack the ware. When the clay is on the wheel, it is the forming, shaping, and creating time. This is when the potter smoothes out all difficult spots to create something new. The clay starts out just a ball of clay, and then it is molded into something beautiful. The clay is transformed in the fire to achieve the durability of the pottery.

Isaiah 64:8 (NIV) says, "Yet, O LORD, you are our Father. We are the clay, you are the potter; we are all the work of your hand." This is what God done for me He came into my life and molded me into my purpose, my destiny. He took on the job of fathering me; I was a marred vessel that needed much tender, loving care. Only God could renew me; only he could make me over again. When I opened my heart unto him and surrendered my will unto the Father, He took out everything that was impure; every yoke that bound me up, He destroyed them. God transformed me in my spirit, soul, and body. My heavenly Father made me new.

2 Corinthians 5:17 (KJV) says, "Therefore if any man be in Christ, he is a new creature: old things are passed away; behold all things are become new." We must go through the same process as the clay. God the Father is the potter, and we are the clay. He removes the impurities out of our life. The Father is the only one who can work on us; He works not only on the outside but also on the inside. God takes a marred vessel and creates something beautiful. God's word pierces through the flaws of our vessel to strip our vessel of all of impurities, all the scars that this world has put on us.

Hebrews 4:12 (KJV) says,

> For the word of God is quick, and powerful, and sharper than any two-edged sword, piercing even to the dividing asunder of soul and spirit, and of the joints and marrow, and is a discerner of the thoughts and intents of the heart.

I had to allow the heavenly Father to get all the junk in me out. I had to let go of all the feelings of being rejected by my dad, all the feelings of being abandoned. When I was a teenager, I remember my mother telling me that my dad wanted her to have an abortion when she was pregnant with me. She told me that she told him she couldn't abort me because she was too far along in her pregnancy. When she told me that, I felt rejected and questioned why was I ever brought into this world when my dad didn't want me. Because my dad rejected me, I felt that I didn't deserve to be loved or accepted by anyone, but deep down within my heart all I wanted was to be loved and accepted.

All my life I felt rejected until I accepted Jesus Christ into my heart. The love of the Father God covered all of the rejection I felt. You may feel rejected and not loved because your dad or mother wasn't in your life, but know that the Father wants to heal you today.

Allow the heavenly Father to make the rough edges in your life straight. Allow Him to purify you of all the issues that you have carried for many years. The Father knows you because He created you and He loves you. Just surrender unto Him everything that eats you to the core. Give Him all your burdens, all your pains, all your troubles, all your disappointments. He knows about your sufferings, and He cares. You are the chosen of God; you are the heir to His promises. Let Him have all the rejection, all the hurt and pain from not having your dad or mother in your life. This is a new day, a new beginning for you! Walk in the acceptance of the heavenly Father.

> And we, who with unveiled faces all reflect the Lord's glory, are being transformed into his likeness with ever-increasing glory, which comes from the Lord, who is the Spirit.
> 2 Corinthians 3: 18 (NIV)

> And we know that all things work together for good to them that love God, to them who are the called according to his purpose.
>
> Romans 8:28 (KJV)

• • • • • • • • • • • • • • •

A Renewed Relationship: Transform into the Father's child. Write your feelings about how you felt because of the severed relationship from your dad. Then talk to your heavenly Father about all your hurts, disappointments, everything that you have list that you have struggled with due to you being separate from your dad. God wants to heal you so that you can receive what He has for you. God wants to heal even the person who didn't have their mother in their life. Surrender all to the heavenly Father.

_____

_____

_____

_____

_____

_____

_____

_____

Zadora Covington

A Fatherless Generation

_____

_____

_____

_____

_____

_____

_____

_____

A *transitioning* has taken place in your life. You do not have to seek for your dad any more. Your father, the heavenly Father, is here. Everything you need is in Him. "For ye are all the children of God by faith in Christ Jesus" (Galatians 3: 26, KJV).

Heavenly Father, I pray that the fatherless will accept your invitation to become your sons and daughters of promise. I pray a mind change and a heart transformation take place. I pray that they no longer live like they are fatherless, but they will walk in their true inheritance as sons or daughters of faith in Christ Jesus. This prayer I pray in Jesus name. Amen.

Faith through the Fire

Life brings us all kinds of unexpected situations, but we must know that there is an ending to every struggle. There is an ending to every fire that we go through. The Bible gives us many examples of biblical people who had to trust God to bring them through the fires of life; it was a test of their faith.

I was asked one day why do I use so many scriptures when I write; my answer to that person was because there is life and power in the Word of God. If you can only learn to apply the word to every situation in your life, you can overcome the enemy. For every situation that you go through, the Word of God has a word for it; if applied by faith, you can come through the fire with the victory.

A familiar story in the Scriptures that many Christians teach and preach about is the act of faith by Shadrach, Meshach, and Abednego; they showed us a prime example of how you can stand on the Word of our heavenly Father and watch Him manifest His glory. Daniel 3:18–20, 23–30 (KJV) says:

But if not, be it known unto thee, O king, that we will not serve thy gods, nor worship the golden image which thou hast set up. Then was Nebuchadnezzar full of fury, and the form of his visage was changed against Shadrach, Meshach, and Abednego: therefore he spake, and commanded that they should heat the furnace one seven times more than it was wont to be heated. And he commanded the most mighty men that were in his army to bind Shadrach, Meshach, and Abednego, and to cast them into the burning fiery furnace. And these three men, Shadrach, Meshach, and Abednego, fell down bound into the midst of the burning fiery furnace. Then Nebuchadnezzar the king was astonished, and rose up in haste, and spake, and said unto his counselors, Did not we cast three men bound into the midst of the fire? They answered and said unto the king, True, O king. He answered and said, Lo, I see four men loose, walking in the midst of the fire, and they have no hurt; and the form of the fourth is like the Son of God. Then Nebuchadnezzar came near to the mouth of the burning fiery furnace, and spake, and said, Shadrach, Meshach, and Abednego, ye servants of the most high God, come forth, and come hither. Then Shadrach, Meshach, and Abednego, came forth of the midst of the fire. And the princes, governors, and captains, and the king's counselors, being gathered together, saw these men, upon whose bodies the fire had no power, nor was an hair of their head singed, neither were their coats changed, nor the smell of fire had passed on them. Then Nebuchadnezzar spake, and said, Blessed be the God of Shadrach, Meshach, and

Abednego, who hath sent his angel, and delivered his servants that trusted in him, and have changed the king's word, and yielded their bodies, that they might not serve nor worship any god, except their own God. Therefore I make a decree, That every people, nation, and language, which speak any thing amiss against the God of Shadrach, Meshach, and Abednego, shall be cut in pieces, and their houses shall be made a dunghill: because there is no other God that can deliver after this sort. Then the king promoted Shadrach, Meshach, and Abednego, in the province of Babylon.

Just like Shadrach, Meshach, and Abednego in the fiery furnace, God was concerned about them, and He protected them and brought them out of that fire with no damage to them or their clothes. They went in the fire, but they came out with the victory. King Nebuchnezzar had to acknowledge their God as the true and only Living God. They trusted that God was going to bring them out of that fire, and He did. The fire of the enemy has no power over us! You can go through the fire and stay free if you keep your trust in God. With God on our side, we have victory over the enemy; what the enemy tries to use against us is what makes us strong.

He provides an entrance to our destiny. Through our hurts, pains, disappointments, we can walk into our calling straight into our blessings. Sometimes we must go through fire to get what God has for us. We aren't exempt from trials and tribulations, but God told us that we are more than conquerors.

Romans 8:37 (KJV) **says,** "Nay, in all these things we are more than conquerors through him that loved us." Just like a house being destroyed by fire, nothing is left but the foundation and sometimes the frame of the house. Yet the boards are left burned, torched, and scorched by fire and smoke. The smoke leaves a stain in the wood and a smell that lingers for a long time. When you look at a house that is destroyed, you may think that there is no hope for that house. But there *is* hope because the foundation is left standing. A new house can be rebuilt on that same foundation even after going through the fire.

Life is the same way; after the fires of life have struck us from all directions, we are left with visible stains and scars. Though life keeps on moving, we are still left with the scars, and the stench of pain is still yet there. The evidence of us going through the fire is still there, even after thirty years. The only way for us to truly get healed from the fires of life is to invite the heavenly Father into the situation. When the heavenly Father is finished rebuilding, not even the stench of sin or the evidences of scars will be visible not on the surface or beneath the surface, they will be gone.

A contractor who specializes in rebuilding homes that have been destroyed by a fire has to use a special kind of chemical to conceal the smell of smoke. Even with using chemicals, you can still smell smoke in a house. It only masks the scent; it doesn't completely take away the smell. It is time for people to stop concealing there hurts, their pains—especially the body of Christ.

And he taught them many things by parables, and said unto them in his doctrine, Hearken; Behold, there went out a sower to sow: And it came to pass, as he sowed, some fell by the way side, and the fowls of the air came and devoured it up. And some fell on stony ground, where it had not much earth; and immediately it sprang up, because it had no depth of earth: But when the sun was up, it was scorched; and because it had no root, it withered away. And some fell among thorns, and the thorns grew up, and choked it, and it yielded no fruit. And other fell on good ground, and did yield fruit that sprang up and increased; and brought forth, some thirty, and some sixty, and some an hundred. And he said unto them, He that hath ears to hear, let him hear.

Mark 4:2–9 (KJV)

The sower soweth the word. And these are they by the way side, where the word is sown; but when they have heard, Satan cometh immediately, and taketh away the word that was sown in their hearts. And these are they likewise which are sown on stony ground; who, when they have heard the word, immediately receive it with gladness; And have no root in themselves, and so endure but for a time: afterward, when affliction or persecution ariseth for the word's sake, immediately they are offended. And these are they which are sown among thorns; such as hear the word, And the cares of this world, and the deceitfulness of riches, and the lusts of other things entering in, choke the word, and it becometh unfruitful. And these are they which are sown on good ground; such as

hear the word, and receive it, and bring forth fruit, some thirtyfold, some sixty, and some an hundred.
Mark 4:14–20 (KJV)

In these scriptures it lets us know that we allow our seed to be choked up by the issues in our life. We won't and can't progress forward until we have surrendered all the issues in our heart unto our heavenly Father. We must allow the fire of the Word of God to burn up everything. The Father is concerned with everything we go through. The heavenly Father is the only one that can make us new again, inside and outside.

2 Corinthians 5:17 (KJV) says, "Therefore if anyone is in Christ, he is a new creation: old things have passed away; behold, all things have become new." We must know that there is still hope.

Job 14:1 (KJV) says, "Man that is born of a woman is of few days, and full of trouble." If your dad hasn't been in your life since you were born, know that the heavenly Father has been there even before you were formed in your mother's womb. He created you for his purpose. The heavenly Father knew the trouble your life would encounter before you were born into this world. The heavenly Father has always been there for you!

Romans 8:34 (NLT) says, "Who then will condemn us? No one—for Christ Jesus died for us and was raised to life for us, and he is sitting in the place of honor at God's right hand, pleading for us." The struggles that we have endured are only temporal.

We must know that no matter what trouble we go through, we are not alone. Our heavenly Father is with us every step of the way. Jesus is praying personally for you; He is your propitiator, healer, deliverer, intercessor, and provider. He supplies all our needs. God is in control, and He is able and willing to restore, deliver, revive, and heal us from life's fires. Sometimes the fire is there to burn off things that must be destroyed out of our life. The fires of life are there to help mold us into what the heavenly Father wants us to become, to help us to know that we can overcome.

One of the fires in my life was going through life without my dad; it was very hard for me growing up without a father figure. My mother didn't have her dad in her life, my siblings and I didn't have our dads in our life. I didn't have a dad in my life to teach me what a father is supposed to teach his daughter. You see, society labels men like they don't have a purpose in their home, but they do. God wouldn't have created man if He thought that he couldn't be a key influence in his family, or in his children's life.

When the heavenly Father created man, He made them in his image and his likeness. This means that God has put in them his attributes and every man is created to be a dad, even if he chooses not to be one. A man's mandate from the heavenly Father is to push his children to excellence. He was created by God to love, protect, and teach his children Christian morals and values. It is up to every man to teach their sons and daughters so that they will one day nurture their own children and leave a legacy of holiness and reverence to God. I wrote this book to lead all the fatherless children in the world to their true father, the heavenly Father. God has always been here, waiting on us to allow Him to come in and have sweet communion with Him. The fires in our life are there to increase our faith in our heavenly Father. We must know that the fires of life aren't there to destroy us, but to destroy the things that the Father wants out of our life and draw us closer to Him.

Trust God through the fires of life. List your struggles and then pray, surrender, and trust the heavenly Father for your deliverance. Psalm 37:40 (KJV) says, "And the LORD shall help them, and deliver them: he shall deliver them from the wicked, and save them, because they trust in him."

_____

_____

_____

_____

_____

_____

_____

_____

_____

A Fatherless Generation

_____

_____

_____

_____

_____

_____

_____

_____

_____

Heavenly Father, I pray you give strength to the weak. I pray that they will surrender all to you, because you are their deliverer. I pray Father that they will trust you no matter what situations arise in their life. I pray, Father, that they will not lean onto their own understanding, but they will acknowledge you in everything. You are our Deliverer, Father, and we depend only on you. In Jesus name I pray. Amen.

The Bigger Picture

We live in a society that desires big things. Big flat screen TVs, big SUVs, fancy sports cars, big homes, fancy cell phones, expensive electronic games...well you get the picture. Yet in the spiritual realm, we can't see the bigger picture. We can't see what our heavenly Father wants to do for us and through us. We struggle with trusting God that he will bring us out of them big situations that seem like they are out of control. We look at the situation like it's not fixable. We must learn to trust God for what we can't see. God consecrated me; he separated me from my dad to move me into the purpose that was set on my life. I had to learn how to accept that my dad wasn't in my life.

God sees the bigger picture; he knows the start, middle, and the finishing point in our life. God knew the struggles that I was going to be faced with due to me not having a father in my life. He knew the struggles that I would have to endure. God knows and understands all that we go through in our life. He is willing and able to deliver us when we surrender unto Him.

In Genesis 37, this passage of scripture tells us about Joseph, who was ordained for a great calling on his life.

Joseph was forced from his father and all he knew to a greater purpose. Joseph suffered so much by the hands of his own brothers. He was cast into a pit, then sold to an Ishmaelite for twenty shekels of silver, and taken to Egypt where he was sold to Potiphar, an officer of Pharaoh.

Joseph's master's wife accused him of trying to rape her, and he was put in prison. Even in the midst of all of his sufferings, the Bible tells us that Joseph was still prosperous; everything that was laid into his hands was prosperous. Joseph sufferings molded him into a great man of God. All his suffering was for a greater purpose. He came from his father's house to a pit, from a pit to slavery, from slavery to overseer of his master's house, from overseer of his master's house to prison, from prison to interpreting the dreams of the butler, baker, and Pharaoh. From there, God raised him up to be ruler over all the affairs of the king.

If it wasn't for him suffering by the hands of his jealous brothers, his family wouldn't have food during the famine in the land, and many people could have died of starvation because of the famine. The enemy doesn't show us the bigger picture. He tries to keep us so broken down with our sufferings that we can't see the outcome is victorious. He tries to keep us in darkness, away from the light of our Savior Jesus.

In all of Joseph's sufferings, God had a greater plan one that would provide food for seven years of plenty and seven years of catastrophic famine. Joseph's purpose was greater than him, greater than his sufferings. What he went through was for a greater purpose, a God-given purpose. Joseph's destiny was not with his father and family but in a far away land, where God raised Joseph up to become a ruler that was favored among man, and God blessed and prospered all that was placed in his hands. He received guidance from his heavenly Father in how to rule over the affairs of the king. The outcome was better than the struggles that Joseph went through.

The Father knows what's best for us. I had to look pass all the issue in my life to see the bigger picture. Coming from the gutters of sexual abuse, rape, feeling rejected, and not loved by my dad, God showed me even in my mummified life that He had a purpose for my life. I was running to the world to fill voids in my life. Nothing or no one could fill those voids; only God can. My life was like a mummy that was buried for many years; I was wrapped up in all my issues. I was dying, and my heart was shriveling up. I couldn't see what God wanted to do through my life's darkest moments.

I know now that my life is not my own and God had a greater purpose for my life. God is in the business of turning our darkest moments into blessings, not only for ourselves but to bless others bringing Him glory. He uses our dark shameful moments to bring hope to a dying, lost world. Jesus is our ultimate example of looking at the bigger picture, because what He went through was for a greater purpose, to die for the sins of the world. Our Savior endured so much to reconcile our broken relationship with our heavenly Father. Through Calvary's cross, our relationship to the heavenly Father was restored. Isaiah 53 describes to us what Jesus endured to give us eternal freedom from sin and death and restore our heritage back to our heavenly Father. Jesus came to heal our brokenness and to rebuild our relationship with the Father.

Isaiah 53:1–12 (The Message) says,

> Who believes what we've heard and seen? Who would have thought God's saving power would look like this? The servant grew up before God—a scrawny seedling, a scrubby plant in a parched field. There was nothing attractive about him, nothing to cause us to take a second look. He was looked down on and passed over, a man who suffered, who knew pain firsthand. One look at him and people turned away. We looked down on him, thought he was scum. But the fact is, it was our pains he carried—our disfigurements, all the things wrong with us. We thought he brought it on himself, that God was punishing him for his own failures. But it was our sins that did that to him, that ripped and tore and crushed him—our sins! He took the punishment, and that made us whole. Through his bruises we get healed. We're all like sheep who've wandered off and gotten lost. We've all done our own thing, gone our own way. And God has piled all our sins, everything we've done wrong, on him, on him. He was beaten, he was tortured, but he didn't say a word. Like a lamb taken to be slaughtered and like a sheep being sheared, he took it all in silence. Justice miscarried, and he was led off—and did anyone really know what was happening? He died without a thought for his own welfare, beaten bloody for the sins of my people. They buried him with the wicked, threw him in a grave with a rich man, Even though he'd never

hurt a soul or said one word that wasn't true. Still, it's what God had in mind all along, to crush him with pain. The plan was that he give himself as an offering for sin so that he'd see life come from it—life, life, and more life. And God's plan will deeply prosper through him. Out of that terrible travail of soul, he'll see that it's worth it and be glad he did it. Through what he experienced, my righteous one, my servant, will make many "righteous ones," as he himself carries the burden of their sins. Therefore I'll reward him extravagantly—the best of everything, the highest honors—Because he looked death in the face and didn't flinch, because he embraced the company of the lowest. He took on his own shoulders the sin of the many, he took up the cause of all the black sheep.

Just as our Savior Jesus humbly surrendered his will to His Father to save us, we must forever keep Jesus's ultimate sacrifice as an example unto us to remind us of the Father's mercy and grace and unconditional love. Jesus showed unconditional love while He was nailed to the cross between two sinners. He told the one on the right this day He would see him in paradise. Jesus was still saving and ministering while he was on the cross. Jesus was yet doing the work of His Father. Jesus ministry didn't end on the cross. He's still interceding on our behalf today.

Luke 23:39–43 (KJV) says,

> And one of the malefactors which were hanged railed on him, saying, If thou be Christ, save thyself and us. But the other answering rebuked him,

> saying, Dost not thou fear God, seeing thou art in the same condemnation? And we indeed justly; for we receive the due reward of our deeds: but this man hath done nothing amiss. And he said unto Jesus, Lord, remember me when thou comest into thy kingdom. And Jesus said unto him, Verily I say unto thee, Today shalt thou be with me in paradise.

We must learn to surrender unto the heavenly Father, trusting him that He knows the outcome for everything that we will go through; He sees the bigger picture.

Seeing beyond what you see, walk by faith to see the bigger picture. You are victorious! Think about a time you knew it was nobody but God that did the miraculous for you. When you get pushed into a corner, remember what the heavenly Father did for you. Write that moment down and remind yourself daily that the Father has everything that concerns you under control. 2 Corinthians 5:7 (kjv) says, "For we walk by faith, not by sight."

_____

_____

_____

_____

_____

_____

A Fatherless Generation

Heavenly Father, I pray they will trust you and walk by faith through your word. In Jesus name I pray. Amen.

Behind a Smile

There are many people today, especially in the body of Christ, who are battling with inner struggles on a daily basis. They struggle with not giving in to their fleshly desires, or they struggle with past issues. Behind a smile is a person that tries to hide their true feelings within. There is a battle that goes on in their mind. They want freedom and peace from the thing that has them bound.

I used to think that I wasn't going to ever find true happiness and eternal peace, but I did when I found the heavenly Father and when I truly surrendered all unto Him. Jeremiah 24:6–7 (KJV) says,

> For I will set mine eyes upon them for good, and I will bring them again to this land: and I will build them, and not pull them down; and I will plant them, and not pluck them up. And I will give them an heart to know me, that I am the Lord: and they shall be my people, and I will be their God: for they shall return unto me with their whole heart.

We must pray to the Father to give us a heart to know Him, a heart to serve Him, a heart to obey his will, and a heart to trust Him, even in the midst of our most dry and thirsty times. Even when we can't feel Him near, He is yet here preserving us. The Father wants our whole heart, not half; we can't be that mirror that reflects the image of Christ just on the outside. The inside of our vessels must reflect Christ, too. What does the mirror of your heart show; what does it reflect? Does it reflect the love of God or hatred for the person that caused you pain? Is your heart tainted by the cares of this world?

Mark 4:19 (KJV) says, "And the cares of this world, and the deceitfulness of riches, and the lusts of other things entering in, choke the word, and it becometh unfruitful." Being two-faced in your spirit only causes you to be bound in your walk with Christ. It's time to rise up from defeat! Let go of the weights. Some of the weights on a person are weights that they are putting on themselves. They inhibit themselves from getting their own breakthrough. You see a smile, but on the inside they are screaming for help. They wonder why they make the same mistakes, why they disappoint God, because they still struggle with things within themselves.

With the Christian society looking like they have it all together, it leaves the people that struggle feeling like they can't tell the church how they truly feel or what they struggle with because they have a fear of being judged. The believer sits in the sanctuary with a smile but is hurting on the inside and is screaming to be set free of the things that have them bound. For many years I was that person. I was broken with many scars. I had a smile—well, a mechanical smile. I could smile even when I felt like trash on the inside. I wanted everyone around me to be happy, but on the inside I was like the Titanic, feeling myself sinking and no one there to throw me out a lifeline. The scars of everything negative in my life laid on me heavily like a ton of concrete bricks on my shoulders.

I battled with the feelings of rejection, because my dad wasn't in my life. When I truly came to the heavenly Father, taking off the veil and allowing the heavenly Father to have everything that hit me to the core. That's when He took that smile of shame and replaced it with His love, healing, forgiveness, and acceptance and allowed me to be free of all that I harbored in my heart. The Father wants us to be free. No one in the Bible was bound after Jesus came into their life, but we have so many still bound. It's because they truly haven't surrendered unto the heavenly Father. Behind the smiles are hatred, disappointment, and unforgiveness, and the list can go on and on. Behind the smile is a man or woman, boy or girl, that has inner scars that only the heavenly Father can heal. The person behind the smile is imprisoned by their emotions, struggles, and their fears.

I felt like the woman with the issue of blood; she was a woman that was an outcast because of her illness. The one thing I notice about that woman is that she never gives up on her healing, and she was persistent until she got her healing. Matthew 9:20 says, "And, behold, a woman, which was diseased with an issue of blood twelve years, came behind him, and touched the hem of his garment." The Bible doesn't tell her name, just tells us that she had an issue. She pressed through the crowd to get to Jesus. All it took was a touch, just a touch mixed with faith for her issue to be gone. If we reach out to touch Jesus, he will reach out to us and touch us back and heal us of all our brokenness. We must be just like the woman with her issue of blood; we must be persistent in getting our healing, deliverance, and forgiveness. Persistence creates faith. With faith, every situation in your life will be moved. Hebrews 4:15 (KJV) says, "For we have not an high priest which cannot be touched with the feeling of our infirmities; but was in all points tempted like as we are, yet without sin." The Father sees our struggles. He wants us to know, just like the Israelites in their bondage in slavery by the Egyptians, He sees their afflictions and sent Moses to lead them to freedom. God has given us a way of escape through Jesus, our Savior. Jesus is the only one who can lead us to freedom out of our wilderness.

Don't be like the Israelites; they were in bondage in the wilderness because of their disobedience. They traveled around the wilderness for forty years; they couldn't find their way out, because they wanted to do things their way instead of God's way. There are many of you that the Father has told to let go of issues or surrender them unto him, but you refuse to, and because of your disobedience you are still fighting with those same old habits and sin issues, same old low self-esteem issues, same old rejection issues, and other same old, same old, sad songs. It's time to stop being disobedient and start being obedient to the will of the Father. You are a child of the King; walk in your blessings not in defeat. This is your transitioning period, this is your season, you have been praying to God to heal you, to help you, well let Him do it! Matthew 7:9–11 (KJV) says,

> Or what man is there of you, whom if his son ask bread, will he give him a stone? Or if he ask a fish, will he give him a serpent? If ye then, being evil, know how to give good gifts unto your children, how much more shall your Father which is in heaven give good things to them that ask him?

Healing of the hearts, mind, soul, and body is a good thing to the Father. He wants us to have it; all we have to do is ask him for it in faith! The issues of the past can be the past not our future or our present!

> For the children of Israel walked forty years in the wilderness, till all the people that were men of war, which came out of Egypt, were consumed, because they obeyed not the voice of the LORD: unto whom the LORD sware that he would not shew them the land, which the LORD sware unto their fathers that he would give us, a land that floweth with milk and honey.
> Joshua 5:6 (KJV)

God wants your smile to not only be a reflective of Him on the outside, but also on the inside. This is the season that the Father is tearing down those old wilderness walls and building up vessels of honor that are no longer broken, but are vessels that depict his very image both on the inside and outside. They will be vessels that are crystal clear, that truly reflect Christ. Not the vessels that at first see themselves as a torn, marred image in a mirror that should have only reflected the image of Christ Jesus. Now they will reflect Him. They will be that peculiar people that illuminates to man the reflection of Christ. No more will they be shattered mirrors but a beautiful image that truly reflects the heavenly Father. Their hearts will reflect the Father in forgiveness, love, and obedience unto Him. 1 Peter 2:9(KJV) says, "But ye are a chosen generation, a royal priesthood, an holy nation, a peculiar people; that ye should shew forth the praises of him who hath called you out of darkness into his marvellous light."

2 Timothy 2:19–21(KJV) says,

> Nevertheless the foundation of God standeth sure, having this seal, The Lord knoweth them that are his. And, let every one that nameth the name of Christ depart from iniquity. But in a great house there are not only vessels of gold and of silver, but also of wood and of earth; and some to honour, and some to dishonour. If a man therefore purge himself from these, he shall be a vessel unto honour, sanctified, and meet for the master's use, and prepared unto every good work.

What's the story behind your smile? What image do you see in the mirror? Is the image rejection? Is it fear? Is it failure? Is it hatred? Is it unforgiveness? Allow the Father to give you a new smile. Are you sick of the hidden issues behind your smile that cause you so much pain? Get rid of the fake smile by opening up your heart to the Father and truly surrendering everything to Him! At this moment, think about something in your past, present, or future that's putting a burden on you. Whatever you are feeling at this moment that's causing you pain, write it down. Pray in your heart to give it to the heavenly Father. Don't live your life in defeat. Galatians 5:1(KJV) says, "Stand fast therefore in the liberty wherewith Christ hath made us free, and be not entangled again with the yoke of bondage."

_____

_____

_____

_____

_____

_____

_____

_____

_____

_____

Zadora Covington

A Fatherless Generation

_____

_____

_____

_____

_____

_____

_____

_____

_____

_____

_____

Father God, my prayer for the person reading this pray is that they will walk in liberty, which you purchased for them on the cross by the ransom of your son Jesus Christ, their Lord and Savior. My prayer Father is that they will not allow the yokes of their past or present entangled them any longer. In Jesus name I pray. Amen

Carnality vs. Spirituality

Have you ever noticed how without thinking you did something or said something that you wish you never had said or done? Well, that's how it is when you don't walk in the Spirit of the heavenly Father. You will constantly operate in your own will instead of the Father's will. You will struggle with your flesh, your uncontrollable desires, and you won't be able to truly do the will of the Father. You will be led by what you feel and not by the guidance of the Holy Spirit. You will do contrary to what God wants you to do, what you know is right to do.

In Romans 7, Paul gives us a prime example of the struggles in the flesh.

> For we know that the law is spiritual: but I am carnal, sold under sin. For that which I do I allow not: for what I would, that do I not; but what I hate, that do I. If then I do that which I would not, I consent unto the law that it is good. Now then it is no more I that do it, but sin that dwelleth in me. For I know that in me (that is, in my

flesh,) dwelleth no good thing: for to will is present with me; but how to perform that which is good I find not. For the good that I would I do not: but the evil which I would not, that I do. Now if I do that I would not, it is no more I that do it, but sin that dwelleth in me. I find then a law, that, when I would do good, evil is present with me. For I delight in the law of God after the inward man: But I see another law in my members, warring against the law of my mind, and bringing me into captivity to the law of sin which is in my members. O wretched man that I am! who shall deliver me from the body of this death? I thank God through Jesus Christ our Lord. So then with the mind I myself serve the law of God; but with the flesh the law of sin.

> Romans 7:14–25 (KJV)

For one to truly walk in the spirit of God, one must first deny himself/herself. Not fulfilling the lustful desires of their flesh, not walking by their own fleshly desires. They must walk circumspectly before the heavenly Father. When you walk in the Spirit, it's like being blindfolded; you can't see your way, but you trust the person who is leading you to help guide you in the right direction and protect you from all obstacles. Being led by the Spirit of the Father is the same way when you allow the Spirit of God to guide you; you will be protected from all things. Romans 8:4–15 (KJV) says,

> That the righteousness of the law might be fulfilled in us, who walk not after the flesh, but after

the Spirit. For they that are after the flesh do mind the things of the flesh; but they that are after the Spirit the things of the Spirit. For to be carnally minded is death; but to be spiritually minded is life and peace. Because the carnal mind is enmity against God: for it is not subject to the law of God, neither indeed can be. So then they that are in the flesh cannot please God. But ye are not in the flesh, but in the Spirit, if so be that the Spirit of God dwell in you. Now if any man have not the Spirit of Christ, he is none of his. And if Christ be in you, the body is dead because of sin; but the Spirit is life because of righteousness. But if the Spirit of him that raised up Jesus from the dead dwell in you, he that raised up Christ from the dead shall also quicken your mortal bodies by his Spirit that dwelleth in you. Therefore, brethren, we are debtors, not to the flesh, to live after the flesh. For if ye live after the flesh, ye shall die: but if ye through the Spirit do mortify the deeds of the body, ye shall live. For as many as are led by the Spirit of God, they are the sons of God. For ye have not received the spirit of bondage again to fear; but ye have received the Spirit of adoption, whereby we cry, Abba, Father.

The scriptures Romans 7:14–25 (KJV) and Romans 8:4–15 (KJV) tell us about living a life of carnality. When we are led by our flesh, we are living a defeated life. Only the ones who are led by the Spirit of the Father are His sons and daughters. We must be Spirit led, not flesh led. When we are carnal-minded, we don't have a sense of direction;

we are led in every direction by our desires. We don't see stop signs, yield signs; we don't see flashing caution lights, and we don't see the signs that say, "Beware, danger is up ahead." Flesh is greedy for self-satisfaction. Flesh has to be gratified. Flesh wants what it wants. It won't stop until it gets what it wants. That's why we must mortify the deeds of the flesh. We must kill all fleshly desires. The only way to mortify our members is to mediated on the Word of God, apply it to our life, stay in sweet communion with the Father, and fast to mortify the flesh. When we fast, the flesh weakens, and the spirit man is strengthened.

In Galatians 5 (KJV), it lets us know that the fruit of the Holy Spirit are love, joy, peace, longsuffering, kindness, goodness, faithfulness, gentleness, and self-control. When I accepted Jesus into my heart, it was a start of Him destroying all the fruits of the flesh in my life. It was a new beginning, a start of my Father teaching me how to love after stripping me of all the hatred that I built up in my heart for so many years. The love of the Father uncovered all the hidden things in my life. The light of the Savior shined down on my brokenness and filled me with unconditional love, love that forgives. The heavenly Father showed me true love by His Son's undying love for me; Jesus's atonement on the cross showed me how to truly forgive and love.

In my first book, My Spiritual Journey into God's Presence, I talk about the sexual abuse and rape that I endured. I know that it was through the love of my heavenly Father that I was able to forgive my abusers. I can't tell you that it was easy, but with God's unfailing love, support, and strength I was able to surrender all unto Him, and the Father brought me through it. The Father gave me peace in the midst of dealing with my past. Unforgiveness is one of the greatest causes of spiritual stagnation. Living a life not forgiving is living a life of carnality, because flesh doesn't want to forgive. It hinders the Father from producing His fruitful gifts into the lives of the believer. Only pure hearts can receive the blessings of the Father. Hearts full of unforgiveness only bind up a person.

> Or else how can one enter into a strong man's house, and spoil his goods, except he first bind the strong man? And then he will spoil his house.
> Matthew 12:29 (KJV)

This scripture lets us know that the only way the enemy can spoil our goods (mind) is if we allow him to bind us. That's the problem with most people; they allow the enemy to play fiddle with their minds. Once the enemy finds a way to enter into your thoughts, he will play on your emotions. Once he finds a way in, he will keep pushing you until he binds you up then he destroys you by attacking you in the mind. The first thing the adversary attacks is our mind because if he can gain entry in our mind he can bind us up. The enemy attacks the mind because he knows its power in suggestive words. What he speaks to us have power to sway us either to do what is suggested or to do the opposite of what he suggests.

The adversary comes to bind up them that are strong in the Lord; that's why you need to guard the gifts that the heavenly Father gives you. Proverbs 4:23 (KJV) says, "Keep thy heart with all diligence; for out of it are the issues of life."

At this moment, if there is anything in your heart that you have unforgiveness about, take this invitation from the heavenly Father to surrender it unto Him. You can't truly walk in the Spirit of the heavenly Father with unforgivness in your heart. Right now, if you will surrender it unto the heavenly Father, He will heal you. God has predestined this moment for you to be set free from the bondage you are in. This is a divine appointment between you and your heavenly Father, receive your healing, receive your breakthrough. No matter what it is, God is able to free you from it. We must learn to let go of the things that trouble us.

I can't stress the importance of having a heart free of the issues of this world enough. No matter what reason you may have for harboring something in your heart, it still isn't a good enough reason. Let go of what has been tormenting you and feel God's love overtake you. The only way the heavenly Father can help you is by you surrendering all to Him. Unforgiveness hinders your prayers. God wants you to know that you don't have to walk in unforgiveness, but you can walk in the Spirit where there is liberty. Come from underneath that bondage; be free in your heart, soul, and body. To truly walk in the Spirit you must lay aside all things. Hebrews 12:1 says,

> Wherefore seeing we also are compassed about with so great a cloud of witnesses, let us lay aside every weight, and the sin which doth so easily be-

set us, and let us run with patience the race that is set before us. You are your own worst enemy.

Surrender all today. I pray a release in your heart today. I pray now that every heart that is defiled by past issues or present issues will be healed and delivered now in the name of Jesus. I renounce every spirit of rejection and unforgiveness over your life, caused by you not having your father or mother in your life. I decree and declare this day that you will walk into the acceptance of the heavenly Father.

Now that you are free of the things that had a death grip on your heart, you can walk freely in the Spirit of the heavenly Father. Don't look back at yesterday. Psalm 42:1 (KJV) says, "As the hart panteth after the water brooks, so panteth my soul after thee, O God."

In the Dake Annotated Reference Bible, it explains how a hart is fond of feeding near the waters. When hunted he will take to the river and stay submerged as long as his breath permits, then swim downstream in the middle so as not to touch the branches. We must stay hungry for the Spirit of God, just like the hart pants after the river. The river symbolizes the Spirit of the Father. When we stay submerged in the presence of God, we will stay free from the weights and sin that so easily beset us.

The fruits of the Spirit will flow in our life. We will be led by the Spirit of God and not by our flesh. Our trust and assurance will be in the Father and not in ourselves or no one else. We must keep a thirst for the presence of the Father. Only our heavenly Father can quench our thirst.

Read Psalm 63 (KJV); this chapter in Psalms gives us an example through David's own experience while he was in the wilderness. David still thirsted for God, he yet sought for the Spirit of God in a dry and thirsty land. It might feel at this moment in your life that you are in a dry and thirsty land, but know that even in the darkest of places God is still there waiting on you to surrender your all unto Him. Psalm 51:11 (KJV) says, "Cast me not away from thy presence; and take not thy holy spirit from me." Our soul should follow close to God. We should be glued to the mercy seat of the heavenly Father.

Read Psalm 42:8 (KJV); in this scripture David talks about how the Lord pours out His unfailing love upon him each day. God's spirit gives life to them that are dead in spirit. Walking in the Spirit of the Father is being a humble discipline individual who walks closely by the Father meditating on His Word and walking in all His ways, being subject only to Him. Living a life undefiled not only shows the Father that we love Him, it also shows Him that we reverence Him for who He is. Walking in the Spirit of the Father, one must walk in the love of the Father. Spirit-led people are people of integrity; they are not prideful or arrogant. They walk by faith and not by sight. They are worshippers, intercessors, and soul winners. Being spirit led, we are conscious of everything we do and say. A person who is spirit led delights in the law of the Lord. They seat at the Master's feet, anticipating a word from Him. The will of the heavenly Father is their will.

Everything about a person changes when they are Spirit led, and not fleshly led. They are no longer controlled by their worldly desires. The law of the Spirit of life in Christ Jesus makes them free from sin and death. The heavenly Father sent His own Son in the likeness of sinful flesh, and for sin, to condemn sin in the flesh.

Romans 8:3 (KJV) says, "For what the law could not do, in that it was weak through the flesh, God sending his own Son in the likeness of sinful flesh, and for sin, condemned sin in the flesh."

The righteousness of the law can now be fulfilled in us, meaning since Christ Jesus our Lord condemned sin in the flesh we can live a life free from sin, walking after the Spirit, not the flesh. We are not saved by the law but are saved through faith in our Lord Jesus. Know that we are not bound by the law but are led by the Spirit. Spirit-led people are concern with the things of the Father God, not the fleshly desires.

To be led by the Spirit of God is to be a faith walker. If you are spirit led, you won't allow situations to detour you; you will stay in the will of the Father. We must stay on course with the Holy Spirit and allow the Spirit of the Father to navigate us through life here on earth to our eternal home in glory. To truly be free of the issues of this world, we must walk in the Spirit of God. The more time we spend with the Father, the more we will give him our problems when they arise in our life. The Father wants us to depend on Him and not ourselves.

List what's in your heart and release it unto the heavenly Father today. He cares all about your situation. He wants to deliver you, just surrender all unto Him. Stay free in the Spirit of God: don't walk in carnality.

Examine your life at this moment; write down every road block in your life that is hindering you from walking in true liberty in the heavenly Father. Declare this day that nothing on your list will stop you from walking in liberty of the Spirit of God. The Father is calling you to liberty. 2 Corinthians 3:17 (KJV) says, "Now the Lord is that Spirit: and where the Spirit of the Lord is, there is liberty."

_____

_____

_____

_____

_____

_____

_____

_____

_____

_____

_____

A Fatherless Generation

Father God, I pray that this person will chose to walk in your liberty, rather than stay in the bondage of their flesh. I pray Father that they will walk a circumspective lifestyle in Christ Jesus. In Jesus name I pray. Amen.

A True Heritage

When we think about heritage, we think about being born into a particular family or social class. We don't have a choice what particular family or social class we were born into; it was predestined before we were born. Some people were born into a family that had wealth; others were born into a family of poverty. Regardless of what family you were born into, you will still be left with a family legacy.

A legacy is not just receiving a financial blessing from a loved one after they have passed; it can be a legacy of a family sharing traditions or sharing the gospel of Jesus Christ from generation to generation. It can also be a legacy of generational sin curses. In the biblical days, the father would give the best birthright to the eldest son in the family. The eldest son of the family looked for the day that he would receive the highest blessings from his father. In the biblical days, to not receive the father's heritage, the firstborn would have to be a profane person.

An example of a generational sin curse or a profane person is Cain. He was the first born of Adam and Eve. Cain's occupation was a tiller of the ground, meaning he was a farmer. He had a brother named Abel; he was a keeper of sheep. The two brothers gave offerings to God. God respected Abel's offering, the firstling of his flock, and not Cain's offering, the fruit of the ground. Cain assassinated his brother because of jealousy and anger. Cain became a fugitive and vagabond in the earth, and the Lord set a mark upon Cain lest anyone finding him should kill him. Because of his sin, a mark was placed upon him; his sin affected him, and it also affected his generation of children after him.

Cain's sin affected his fourth generation. Lamech was Cain's great-great-great-great grandson. Lamech slayed two men, and he told his wives that if Cain shall be avenged sevenfold for murder, he will be avenged seventy and sevenfold. Cain missed out on his birthright to Adam because of his sin. Adam missed out on enjoying the blessings of the heavenly Father because he ate of the forbidden fruit of the tree that God told him not to eat. Adam was driven out of the Garden of Eden because of disobedience and his sin. Cain was driven from the face God, just like his father Adam, because of sin. The seed was in Adam, and it transferred to Cain. Adam lost the birthright from the heavenly Father, and Cain lost his father Adam's birthright, and Lamech didn't receive a birthright from his father, Methusael.

After Adam and Eve had lost two sons, they had another one and name him Seth. Seth received the blessings that Cain would have received, because the Bible tells us that Seth called upon the name of the Lord. Adam gave his generation of children a legacy of generational sin curses. Read Genesis 4. An example of receiving a birthright from a father is in Genesis 25:29–34 (KJV); this passage of Scripture talks about Esau promising his birthright to his twin brother, Jacob, for stew meat. Esau was a profane man, because he chose the stew meat over his rights to his father's inheritance. Esau chose to feed his hunger rather than receive a legacy gift from his father, Isaac. It was an irreverent act on Esau's part.

The inheritance is the firstborn's birthright bestowed upon them at birth and shouldn't be treated as something common. We shouldn't treat the gift of becoming children of God as something common. To be called a child of the heavenly Father is a privilege; not everyone is called, and few are chosen.

Matthew 20:16 (KJV) says, "So the last shall be first, and the first last: for many be called, but few chosen."

Esau rejected the birthright of Isaac his Father, because he treated a blessing as something defiled by giving it away for some meat. If it was important to him, or even meant something to him, or if he even knew what he was truly receiving, he would have never sold his birthright. Esau could've been the father of a great tribe of children, but he gave up his blessing for some meat; therefore Jacob becomes the father of twelve sons that became the tribes of Israel. A nation grew from the twelve sons of Jacob.

That's the blessing of walking in the heritage of the heavenly Father. We as children of God must stop treating our heritage as something of no importance. We must know what we truly have received when we became children of the heavenly Father. We mustn't take for granted the heritage we have with our heavenly Father. We share the gospel with many people, and yet we still struggle to have faith in it; we still yet struggle to live the life of holiness and reverence to the heavenly Father.

Esau allowed his fleshly desires to cause him to miss out on his blessings. Genesis 27 (KJV) lets us know that Isaac gave Jacob Esau's birthright. Due to Isaac being blind, he gave Esau's birthright to Jacob. The blessing was Esau's, but Jacob stole Esau's blessing from him by imitating him before Isaac. The stolen blessing caused feuding amongst brothers. Often we have preferred to accept a quick fix, a substitute for the real thing. We have rejected the invitation to become the sons and daughters of God. We have been rejecting our true birthright, our true heritage.

For so long we have allowed the enemy to steal our birthright, we have walked in the wrong inheritance, and we have been an inheritance to the wealth of sin that leads to eternal damnation, eternal death. The inheritance of sin reaps death. A sinner's legacy is passed down from generation to generation. Exodus 20:5 (KJV), "Thou shalt not bow down thyself to them, nor serve them: for I the Lord thy God am a jealous God, visiting the iniquity of the fathers upon the children unto the third and fourth generation of them that hate me."

The only way to break the legacy of sin's curse off of one's life is to accept Jesus Christ into your heart and put on His nature. 2 Corinthians 5:17 (KJV) says, "Therefore if any man be in Christ, he is a new creature: old things are passed away; behold, all things are become new."

When I truly accepted the will of God that my dad wasn't in my life for a reason, that's when I began to learn and understand the blessings of being a child of the heavenly Father. There are so many blessings that we reap because we are children of the living God. Romans 8:14–19 (KJV) says,

> For as many as are led by the Spirit of God, they are the sons of God. For ye have not received the spirit of bondage again to fear; but ye have received the *Spirit of adoption*, whereby we cry, Abba, Father. The Spirit itself beareth witness with our spirit, that we are the children of God: *And if children, then heirs; heirs of God, and joint-heirs with Christ;* if so be that we suffer with him, that we may be also glorified together. For *I reckon that the sufferings of this present time are not worthy to be compared with the glory which shall be revealed in us.* For the earnest expectation of the creature waiteth for the manifestation of the sons of God.

The only way to inherit the blessings of the Father God is by receiving Christ Jesus as your Lord and Savior and then staying in sweet communion with the Word of God. Through the Word of God, we get to know God as the sovereign Father. John 14:6 (KJV) says, "Jesus saith unto him, I am the way, the truth, and the life: no man cometh unto the Father, but by me."

False religions like Buddhism, Hinduism, Islam, and Confucianism along with all other false religions are telling people that they have what we need. They offer a fake imitation of the real God. They give false hopes, but Jesus gives us hope, forgiveness, and salvation in Him. Jesus is the only way to the Father God. Every other way is counterfeit.

Buddhism, Hinduism, Islam, and other erronious teachings give us false religion, not a true relationship with the heavenly father. Jesus gives us a relationship, not religion.

Our Jesus was crucified for our sins to fix our broken relationship with our heavenly Father, not to give us religion. Jesus was a propitiation for our sins to restore our broken relationship back to the Father. The false religions like Muslim, Buddhism, Hinduism, and Confucianism worship different fake gods who can't have a personal relationship with you; they can't be touched for your infirmities. Hebrews 4:15 (KJV) says, "For we have not an high priest which cannot be touched with the feeling of our infirmities; but was in all points tempted like as we are, yet without sin."

Only Jesus knows how you truly feel, because He is the only one who has been touched by your infirmities. He has borne your sins so that you wouldn't have to. He cares, and only through Him we are given another chance to have a personal relationship with our heavenly Father.

John 14:1–3 (KJV) lets us know that Jesus has a prepared place for a prepared people. Only the true heirs of God will receive eternal life where they will live forever with Jesus. The promise for eternal life is only for the believers of Jesus Christ. Jesus teaches a parable about the ten virgins five was wise and five was foolish. The foolish virgins weren't prepared for the bridegroom to come get them. They were left behind because they weren't preparing themselves for the coming of their bridegroom. Many people today prepare themselves in the natural but not in the spiritual. They have the lifestyle of religion down pack, but they down have a true relationship in their hearts with the Father. They miss out on the whole point of being a follower of Jesus Christ. It's not in religion, but relationship. People look for God in all the wrong places, instead of looking for him where He abides in their hearts.

Read John 10:1–18 (KJV). The false religions teach people that there are other routes they can go through to get to the heavenly Father, but they are wrong. Jesus Christ is the only way to the Father. Jesus said that any other way is a thief and a robber. The scribes and Pharisees of our day are the false religions that try to eliminate Christ Jesus from the Father. The scribes and Pharisees of biblical times are a prime example of how people try to get to the Father by their own religion. The scribes and Pharisees were religious people. They had a form of godliness, but they denied Jesus as the Lord and Savior of the world.

Read Matthew 5:20 (KJV). This passage of scripture lets us know that our righteousness must exceed theirs or we will not enter His kingdom. The scribes and Pharisees were ritualistic in their lifestyle; they knew the law but not God.

The false religions give false hopes. They give society a false assurance and temporarily fill a void in people life. People need to know that there is true hope, and that hope is in Jesus Christ alone. No one else can give you what you yearn for. People have tried so many false religions; it's time to tear down all those filthy shrines that have no power to heal, deliver, restore, or set free. The Bible says in John 8:32–36 (KJV),

> And ye shall know the truth, and the truth shall make you free. They answered him, We be

> Abraham's seed, and were never in bondage to any man: how sayest thou, Ye shall be made free? Jesus answered them, Verily, verily, I say unto you, Whosoever committeth sin is the servant of sin. And the servant abideth not in the house for ever: but the Son abideth ever. If the Son therefore shall make you free, ye shall be free indeed.

This passage of scriptures lets us know when we know the truth we will be made free from the power of sin and death. Many people are in bondage because they don't know the truth. They let everyone else tell them what truth is instead of them studying and researching the truth for themselves. 2 Timothy 2:15 (KJV) says we must study the word of God and rightly understand God's word. We must know God's word in order to know His will for us. When false teachers and false doctrine is presented to us we will know the truth and we won't accept phony doctrine. The word of God is alive and has power. False doctrine or religion is a stronghold that traps people to control them. John 8:32–36 (KJV) lets us know that those that know the truth and accept the truth are made free. Many are bound, because they won't accept the truth of the Gospel of Jesus. People who refuse to hear the truth get wrapped up in the bondage of all kinds of doctrine and religion. We were created to be free; we were created to walk in liberty of the Father, but many would rather be enslaved to man's teachings that are false.

Now we know that if we are not children of the heavenly Father, we are servants of sin (verse 34) and not heirs to the promise. The blessing of being the children of the

Father is that we are free through King Jesus our Lord, and we are heirs of the promises. The heavenly Father wants a relationship with us, not a ritual experience of worship and religious acts. He wants intimacy with us. The Father is calling people from all walks of life, from all the four corners of the world, whom He has called to be sons and daughters of the promise. It is time for you to receive the promises of the Father; they are for you! Psalm 78 (KJV) says,

> Give ear, O my people, to my law: incline your ears to the words of my mouth. I will open my mouth in a parable: I will utter dark sayings of old: *Which we have heard and known, and our fathers have told us. We will not hide them from their children, shewing to the generation to come the praises of the* LORD, *and his strength, and his wonderful works that he hath done.* For he established a testimony in Jacob, and appointed a law in Israel, which he commanded our fathers, that they should make them known to their children: That the generation to come might know them, even the children which should be born; who should arise and declare them to their children: That they might set their hope in God, and not forget the works of God, but keep his commandments: And might not be as their fathers, a stubborn and rebellious generation; a generation that set not their heart aright, and whose spirit was not steadfast with God.

The Father is raising up a generation of believers who will say, enough is enough; all I want is a true experience with the heavenly Father. Building up the same old shrines of religion just won't do for this new generation of believers. This new generation will be able to tap into God's glory; they will operate upon a faith that is unwavering built upon the Word of God. The plain old types of services that they have experience just won't do for them; they want an intimate experience with God.

The atmosphere will be an atmosphere full of worship to the Father; they will truly know Him as their heavenly Father and reverence Him for who He is and not just for what He does. They will be a generation of believers who set the atmosphere for God to come in and manifest His glory to bless those who are in the place. Intimacy is what God wants from you and me. We must crave his presence. This generation will come clean with God and man, meaning they won't hide their sin because they want nothing but God; they want nothing but righteousness and holiness. They want to have a submerging experience into His Glory.

This generation of believers are saying what Psalm 51:11 (KJV) says, "Cast me not away from thy presence; and take not thy holy spirit from me." We must not only exemplify Him in our outer appearance, we must have His nature. Our light must illuminate to the world that we are believers of Jesus Christ. The Father is doing the separating; no more will the world have to guess who the children of God is.

Matthew 13:30 (KJV) says, "Let both grow together until the harvest: and in the time of harvest I will say to the reapers, Gather ye together first the tares, and bind them in bundles to burn them: but gather the wheat into my barn." The Father is pouring out His Spirit upon those who are truly thirsty. This generation of believers won't settle for the same old dried-up religion that wants you to have a form of godliness.

2 Timothy 3:5 (KJV) says, "Having a form of godliness, but denying the power thereof: from such turn away." It's now time for the true believers to stand strong and go to battle, for us and our future generation of children. We must leave them a legacy of living a life of holiness and righteous consecrated unto our heavenly Father.

Which heritage do you have? Is it a heritage of our heavenly Father or a heritage of a sin curse? Receive your true heritage now!

If you grew up without your dad in your life, you know how it feels to be fatherless. Think about how you felt not having your dad in your life. I felt rejection because I didn't have my dad in my life. Now take out the time to mediate over what you read in this chapter. When you are a child of the Most High God, the key point that I want you to draw from this chapter is that you can receive a spiritual heritage. I didn't have a heritage from my dad, but I do have one with my heavenly Father. What does it mean to you to have a true heritage with the heavenly Father? Write it down. If you haven't yet received Jesus as your Lord and Savior, pray this prayer.

Lord Jesus, I acknowledge and confess that I am a sinner. Forgive me of my sins; purify my heart, mind, and body. Help me to live for you. Come in my heart and be the Lord of my life. Amen. Once you have prayed this prayer to the heavenly Father, now you are walking in your true heritage as a child of the heavenly Father. Every promise in the Bible is for you.

Zadora Covington

A Fatherless Generation

_____

_____

_____

_____

_____

_____

_____

_____

_____

_____

_____

_____

Acts 2:39 (KJV) says, "For the promise is unto you, and to your children, and to all that are afar off, even as many as the LORD our God shall call."

The Father's Unfailing Love

Love is a four-letter word that is used so freely. People are so quick to tell someone I love you, but is their love unconditional? What is their love built upon? Is it selfish love? What are their motives for giving love? What are the strings attached to their love?

Everyone gives love, looking to receive love back in return or something else. Sometimes what they call love is not actually love at all, but it is selfish affections that they give to gain what they are trying to receive from someone. Love is something given without looking for something in return, with no strings attached. The Father's love has no conditions, no limitations or strings attached to his love. He loved us even when we didn't love Him back. There is no contract we must sign to receive God's love, no stipulations. The Father's love has no restrictions. The Father loves us even in our sinful state. God gives His love freely. Even when we receive the free gift of salvation from Jesus, we are getting a gift with no strings attached. He exchanges our sins and shames for forgiveness and love, and we become a new creation in Him; no more do we have to be labeled for what we used to do.

2 Corinthians 5:17 (KJV) says, "Therefore if any man be in Christ, he is a new creature: old things are passed away; behold, all things are become new."

Many times we have seen someone who was an alcoholic, and when they became sober everything about them changed, their attitude, their actions; everything about them is different. This is how a person is when they truly accept Jesus in their heart, he forgives them of all their sinful ways and teaches them how to live a life of holiness and righteousness unto Him. They are like night and day. The heavenly Father is the only one who can change your night into day. He is the only one who can make you a new creation.

> When Jesus heard it, he saith unto them, They that are whole have no need of the physician, but they that are sick: I came not to call the righteous, but sinners to repentance.
> Mark 2:17 (KJV)

Read Hosea 1 in its entirety. In this particular scripture, there was a prophet named Hosea; he was the prophet for the Northern Kingdom of Israel. God told him to marry a prostitute named Gomer. She left him for a life of prostitution. God used the struggles of the prophet Hosea with his prostitute wife to show His unconditional love toward Israel. No matter how many times Gomer committed adultery, Prophet Hosea still loved her unconditionally. Gomer had children by other men, but Prophet

Hosea still loved her. Prophet Hosea paid fifteen pieces of silver, five bushels of barley, and a measure of wine to get his wife back. He must have had unconditional love for his wife to have not forsaken her and to pay to get her back. The heavenly Father was forgiving, faithful, caring, kind, and loving toward the Israelites even though they left Him. He still rained blessings down on them.

So many times we leave the Father to adventure into the sin of darkness. God was teaching us through Hosea's life struggles that His mercies are sufficient. The Father loved the Israelites beyond their greatest expectations; God's love is much deeper than what their mind could fathom. The prophet Hosea's love for his prostitute wife and his forgiveness of her adulterous lifestyle is symbolic of the Father's love to the Israelites and their adulterous affair with the world. Israel was untrue to God; they openly committed adultery by worshipping false gods.

They swapped the glory of God for the ignominy of forbidden objects of worship. They fellowship with people with immoral nature and they started picking up their bad habits. While they were faithless, straying away, being sinful, rebellious, disobedient, and not desiring to please God, He still yet showed them faithfulness, mercy and grace, kindness, lovingness, and compassion. Every time they came running back to the Father when they needed Him, and the Father still yet accepted them back and love them.

By God showing His love to them it transformed them; it drew them to repentance and obedience. The Father's love is unfeigned. God paid the ultimate price for humanity. He gave his only Son to pay our sin debt. Just like the prophet paid fifteen pieces of silver, five bushels of barley, and a measure of wine to buy back his wife. The Father said, "My love is so great that I'm willing to put my son Jesus up for a ransom for humanity."

Jesus is the sacred wine poured out for the sins of the world. Our heavenly Father sacrificed His son in faith, knowing that someone will come to repentance and drink of the cup of salvation. The sacrifice of our heavenly Father's only begotten Son Jesus showed great love and faith. When we give our last for a purpose we still have doubts that it will bring forth a return. The Father didn't worry if there was going to be one or a billion who would receive salvation, He just gave His only son Jesus Christ for a ransom for our sin debt, not worrying about how many would receive the gift of eternal life.

Even in my life I look at how the Father could take me and love me and adopt me as His own. Not only did He change my whole genetic makeup by saving me and giving me a new nature, but He also gave me a new inheritance; I became the heir to everything that was His. His love for me drew me to Him. His love drew me to repentance and acceptance of Him fathering me. We all were an adulterous generation, a doomed generation lost until the salvation of our Lord Jesus came to save us.

You may ask yourself how God can love someone like you. Well, I can tell you, if He can accept me when I was doing all my sins, I know He will accept you. You may ask why the heavenly Father would want to be a father to us. The Father's love covered all our sins. We are precious to Him, because he created us in His own image and likeness and gave us dominion over everything.

Read Genesis 1:26–27 (KJV). God's love doesn't have any favoritism; he loves everyone. No matter what you have done, He still loves you. God has set His acceptance and approval over our lives in the beginning when He created the first man and woman. If you have any doubt about the love of the heavenly Father, search the pages of the Bible. Every book of the Bible tells about God's love for you. The Bible is a love book to you from the Father. The Bible will lead you to your eternal home to the heavenly Father.

You shouldn't have any doubt after you have read the story of how the prophet Hosea loved his wife the prostitute so much that he never gave up on her, or after reading about how the Father gave his only begotten Son, Jesus, for a propitiation for your sins. This act of love should show you that you are loved, accepted, called, and approved by the Father. The Father won't and can't give up on you if you won't give up on yourself. Just like the prostitute wife received love even though she was an adulterer, we still receive the love of the Father. He can't hate, because He is love, and He wouldn't hate what He created after His image, because we are in the image of Him.

The Father doesn't hate you; He hates sin and what it does to you. The sin separates you from the Father. You see, God loves you no matter what. Yes, of course there are consequences for sin, which is death, but the Father still loves us and gives everyone an escape from sin death by His Son, Jesus Christ. Now when you think, feel, or someone tells you God doesn't love you, remember that it's not true; the Father loves you no matter what His love is unfailing and unfeigned.

• • • • • • • • • • • • • •

Think about areas in your life that you feel unloved because you didn't have a dad in your life. Write down those things and tell yourself God's love and forgiveness will cover those things. Look at your list and know that what's on this list don't relate to you anymore, because you have repented and given it to Him and it's been covered in the blood of Jesus.

_____

_____

_____

_____

_____

_____

_____

_____

_____

_____

A Fatherless Generation

John 14:23(KJV) says, "Jesus answered and said unto him, If a man love me, he will keep my words: and my Father will love him, and we will come unto him, and make our abode with him."

Father, I pray that the person reading this prayer right now will allow your love to overtake them. Father, when they feel unloved, I pray they will remember you're unselfish, unconditional love you showed when you gave your son Jesus Christ for a ransom for their sins. I pray that they will forever feel your love that overtakes them daily. In Jesus name I pray. Amen.

No Condemnation

We are the worst bashers, the worst condemners; we are the worst fault finders against ourselves. We condemn ourselves for things that happen five, ten, twenty, or thirty years ago. That thing that condemns us hangs over our head, reminding us that we are guilty and not worthy of pardon.

The spirit of condemnation takes everything from us and it holds a firm death grip on us so that we can't see that the heavenly Father has set His love and approval over us. For years I condemned myself for what my dad did to my family. Even after I had accepted Jesus in my heart, I still blamed myself for everything that my dad did to my mother and siblings. I walked around feeling condemned for many years. It is bad when you allow yourself to carry the weight of what someone else has done. I accepted my dad's wrongs as my own.

Many people are carrying the weights and burdens of other people's issues. If you have been carrying a family secret or just been holding on to an issue for a long time, it is now your time, it is your season to let it go. I can tell you many times I woke up, day in and day out, reliving what my dad had done to my mother and siblings, and blaming myself only made things worst.

God wanted me to write about condemnation, because so many people are allowing things of their past to condemn them. They walk around feeling condemned. They feed into the suggestions of the enemy. The more they are reminded of their past the more condemnation comes, the more they feel rejection, failure, and not forgiveness. The enemy uses their past to cause them to fall into different strongholds. Condemnation is something that many people struggle with. It is time for you to come out of the condemned walls into walls of acceptance, walls that are no more drowned out with sorrow, hurt, pain, disappointment, angry, resentment, rejection, or fear.

This is your season for you to walk into your liberty that you have longed for so many years! It's time for us to stop labeling ourselves as condemned. We are precious in the sight of God. The ground you are on now is not condemned, it is *blessed*! The enemy reminds us of our past to keep us in a condemned state, but we must know who we are in Christ Jesus. The Father wants us to be free in our minds. The enemy reminded me that I was fatherless and that my dad rejected me, and when he was with my mother he wanted her to abort me, but the heavenly Father's love washed away all my hurt and pain of feeling rejected and helped me forgive my dad for what he did to me and my family. God wants us to be free.

Romans 8:1 (KJV) says, "There is therefore now no condemnation to them which are in Christ Jesus, who walk not after the flesh, but after the Spirit." For many years I condemned myself for things that happened to me in my past. I became my own enemy. I didn't see the love and forgiveness of the heavenly Father, because I had allowed myself to see nothing but condemnation. The moment we are accepted into the heavenly Father's royal family, everything about us changes. Our past is gone!

There are many Christians that accept Jesus as their Lord and Savior but don't truly accept that He has forgiven them. They beat themselves up day and night over the same old issues. Some of the issues of life cause condemnation. Some issues are like our old, worn-out clothes in our closet; every now and then we pull them back out trying them on to see if they still fit us; some do and some don't, and if they fit we keep them, and if they don't we sometimes still refuse to get rid of them, hoping that we will lose weight to squeeze into them again one day soon.

What I'm saying is, stop allowing old issues in your closet stop you, drag those old issues out of your closet, ladies and gentlemen; have a rummage close-out sale. Stop trying to cover up the things in your life that bind you up!

Once we truly accepted the Lord in our heart, we were justified by faith. No more condemned into eternal darkness, but given eternal life in Jesus Christ our Lord. What is condemning you is it the rejection of your dad or your mother, the shame of being a victim of sexual abuse, a victim of rape, aborting a baby, homosexuality, or anything that you have done in your past or present that you are ashamed of and feel you can't forgive yourself of or that the heavenly Father won't forgive you for. Know once you have truly accepted Christ Jesus into your heart and purpose in your heart to live for Him and do His will, you are no more condemned. When we surrender our all to the Father, He will heal us of all our brokenness. Now it's time to stop allowing hindrances of past and present situations keep you from walking in the liberty of your heavenly Father.

I'm talking to the elite of God, to them who are ready to stop feeling and being condemned by their past or present issues. The Father is calling you out of your condemned state. The Father told me to say to them that walk out of their condemned state, call them the elite of God, because you are the ones who are stepping out and shaking off those condemned clothes and being clothed with acceptance of the heavenly Father. The elite of the heavenly Father is a small group of people within a larger sector of people who have chosen to not stay in a group with others that are accepting to be condemned from their past or present issues, but they have chosen to walk into the acceptance, forgiveness, and love of the Father.

Romans 3:23–25 (KJV) says,

> For all have sinned, and come short of the glory of God; Being justified freely by his grace through the redemption that is in Christ Jesus: Whom God hath set forth to be a propitiation through faith in his blood, to declare his righteousness for the remission of sins that are past, through the forbearance of God.

At this very moment, if you are relating to what I'm saying about blaming yourself for other people's wrongs or not forgiving your own self, you need to surrender unto the Father and let Him heal you of all the condemnation that you are feeling right at this moment, allow the Father to heal you. The Father has set his approval over you when you were created in your mother's womb, so know you were designed with a purpose and ordained for a calling and anointed for a great and mighty work. We were found guilty, but Jesus has pronounced us innocent through the shedding of His blood for our sins. The Father is in the business of accepting condemned people. The verdict has been announced a long time ago. We have been found not guilty through the *blood of Jesus*. Praise God. The adversary is defeated.

Everything that hits you to the core that condemns you, I want you to declare today, no more will you allow yourself to walk in condemnation.

John 8:36 (KJV), "If the Son therefore shall make you free, ye shall be free indeed."

Walk in the liberty of your heavenly Father! No condemnation! Write down the issues that have been condemning you; make a decree to your adversary (the devil) that no more will he use those issues to put strongholds on your life, and no more will they control you. Today declare it is over, by the power and authority in the blood of Our Lord and Savior, Jesus Christ! *It is over*! You are the elite of the heavenly Father! He has set His approval and love over you!

———————————————————————

———————————————————————

———————————————————————

Zadora Covington

Romans 8:1(KJV) says, "There is therefore now no condemnation to them which are in Christ Jesus, who walk not after the flesh, but after the Spirit."

Father, I pray that the person reading this book will no longer walk a condemn lifestyle, but they will walk in your acceptance and love. In Jesus name I pray. Amen.